TEACHING KIDS TO WRITE

Written by Eleanor W. Hoomes, Ph. D.
Cover Design by James Uttel
Illustrations by Karen Neulinger and James Uttel

ISBN 1-56644-961-8

Table of Contents

Introduction to Teachers

Students are given writing assignments constantly—the ubiquitous essay for English class, the book report in history, the results of an experiment in science. Outside school the need continues for students to write clearly—messages to members of their families, thank-you notes, letters. Some students even write for pleasure—diaries, journals, poems, stories, articles, plays.

Regardless of what students are writing and why, the starting point is always that blank piece of paper that must be filled. To whom are they writing? Why? What do they write? How do they write it? What form do they use? What rules and style do they follow? TEACHING KIDS TO WRITE has been written to assist you in teaching students how to write and to teach them that writing is something that they can do, and, in most cases, do competently.

Students can write, some better than others, that is true, but they can all be taught simple writing skills. Just as all journeys start with the first step, any kind of writing starts with the first word. Students can be taught to combine words into sentences, sentences into paragraphs, and paragraphs into essays and stories.

The trick is very simple. Students write one word at a time. You teach them how to take what they already know and/or what they learn through research and put it on paper word by word, sentence by sentence, and paragraph by paragraph. As a teacher, you get students to think about the component parts of the essay or story and to break down the story into manageable pieces. This way students are not scared wordless by the idea of writing an essay or story.

TEACHING KIDS TO WRITE is designed to help you increase the effectiveness of your teaching of writing. First, you must clarify your goals so that you know exactly what it is you want to achieve with your students. Your time is limited; you need measurable results. Few of your students will be gifted writers; however, all of your students can be taught to write readable prose.

You *can* teach the writing process by approaching it one step at a time. You *can* teach your students to write by having them write regularly. You *can* teach your students to be more observant and to relish the magic of everyday, ordinary people and events. You *can* teach them the significance of language—its power, its various uses, and its beauty. You *can* teach them how to write what they need to write. So, concentrate on what you *can* do and forget what you cannot do with your students. Establish reachable goals and work toward them.

Good writing informs and entertains; often it is intended to persuade. It holds the good reader's interest and pulls the good reader into the world of the writer. It is much easier to be a good reader than it is to be a good writer. It is also often easier to teach writing than it is to write; however, it is not easy for a good teacher to teach good writing without also being a writer. All of which leads to the point I am attempting to make. As a teacher of writing you must also write.

Notice I said write, not publish. Actually, you need to write often in order to keep your writing skills honed, and if what you write is also publishable, that is simply an extra bonus. In any case, you must be capable, even adept, at doing any writing you ask your students to do. So, practice each writing assignment before using it in class. That way your surprises are more likely to be pleasant ones.

TEACHING KIDS TO WRITE, Book I, contains many suggestions to help you organize your writing classes and to help you implement your ideas. It also contains writing activities to use with your students. TEACHING KIDS TO WRITE, Book II, the companion book to TEACHING KIDS TO WRITE, contains more writing activities and suggestions. In addition, you will find a list of other books that I have written listed on the following page. Any of these books may be useful to you while you are teaching writing.

Happy writing!

Eleanor Wolfe Hoomes

Other Books by Eleanor Wolfe Hoomes:

The Create-a-Story Series (8 titles):

CREATE-A-SLEUTH: Writing a Detective Story

CREATE HEROES AND VILLAINS: Writing an Adventure Story

CREATE-A-FANTASY: Writing a Whimsical Story

CREATE-A-FUTURE: Writing a Science Fiction Story

CREATE-A-UTOPIA: Writing an Idealistic Story

CREATE-AN-AUTOBIOGRAPHY: Writing a Personal Story

CREATE-A-COMEDY: Writing a Humorous Story

CREATE-A-MONSTER: Writing a Horror Story

LAUGHING MATTERS

MORE LAUGHING MATTERS

STRAIGHT FROM THE SOURCE: Nine Research Projects

AT THE GRASS ROOTS LEVEL: A Community Research and Write Project

All titles are available from Educational Impressions, Inc., Hawthorne, NJ.

Part I
For Teachers

Teacher Directions

Most students have a large potential for creativity, but by the time students are in the upper elementary grades, too much of their creativity has been submerged by the educational and socialization processes. Learning is central to continuous growth and development. Learning encourages creativity; in fact, learning must be taking place for creativity to flourish.

Creative teachers encourage students to ask questions, change things around, add to or delete from, reorganize, make new connections, and invent and develop new ideas. They gently lead (and if that does not work, they shove gently and then, not so gently) students to ask, to seek, to look, to examine, and to welcome new knowledge, new experiences, new ideas, and new concepts.

Creative teachers welcome flexibility, openness, non-conformity, curiosity, and skepticism. They expect their students to play with ideas, words, and relationships and to experiment with situations and solutions. They expect their students to approach learning with a sense of humor which frees them from the crippling ideas that education and learning are always serious and should always be treated seriously.

Creative writing flourishes in a relaxed, friendly, supportive classroom, a classroom where trust and cooperation are encouraged, and in a classroom as free as possible from distraction, pressure, and frustration. A satisfactory classroom writing ambience must be engineered by you; it is something that can gradually be achieved and maintained, and you must teach your students its value.

Be creative and imaginative when you are planning. You will expect your students to be creative and imaginative when they write; it is only fair that you exercise your creativity and imagination in developing writing assignments for them and in designing their writing environment.

Set up a regular writing time. Once a day, twice a week, every day—it does not matter as long as you and your students honor the schedule and do not deviate from it. Silence during writing time is essential. You might request the office to hold all messages during the predetermined writing time. A sign hung outside on the door might proclaim, "Creative Work Going On" or "Quiet! Writers at Work." (Use those on pages 27 and 28 or make your own.) If writing time is important to you and you make it something special, your students will soon look forward to their writing time as special also.

Allow and encourage students to be free-wheeling, especially while they are in their incubation phase (when they are "hatching" ideas). You might like to teach them brainstorming techniques for use during this period. Oral composition is also useful at this point. (The rules of brainstorming and tips on oral composition follow.)

Writing cannot be divorced from the other subject areas nor can it be divorced from all of life's experiences. Students must have something about which to write, and they also need a basic understanding of the simple mechanics of writing, which they should have by the fourth or fifth grades. Creative writing should help students improve all the language arts skills. Be imaginative and creative first with your students; have students write for pleasure, not grades, at first. Place emphasis on descriptions, feelings, actions, facts, reactions, and thoughts. Then, when students are more comfortable with the task of putting words down on paper, start to deal with mechanics by showing them how correct usage makes their writing more understandable to their audience. Now is the time to gradually start introducing the rules of grammar, punctuation, spelling, dictionary skills, and writing techniques, but only as they are needed to improve the messages of the student writers.

During writing time you might circulate around the room to make sure everyone is writing. When students need help, they may raise their hands and you may go to their desks for quiet consultations, or you might prefer to let them come to you. With students that I know well, I place a chair next to my desk and students come to it when they need help after the writing period has started. I still circulate, but when I see a student in the chair, I give the desired help quietly so as not to disturb the other students. Remember, it is very easy to be distracted and lose a nebulous idea; a fleeting idea once lost is likely lost forever. At other times I complete the writing assignment which the students are doing. If I write as the students are writing, I share my efforts with them when they share their efforts with me and their classmates.

Be as flexible as possible about allowing students to substitute their own ideas for any you use from this book, other sources, or those you develop yourself. Listen to their alternative suggestions; you might be able to use them in developing materials. Sometimes you will be able to improvise on the spot and incorporate students' ideas into your lesson plans for the day. Not all writing assignments should have a predetermined subject; some should be open for students to choose their own topics and styles.

Providing time for writing overruns or giving students extra time to complete writing projects started earlier can become a worrisome situation. You want to be fair, but, face it, there are students who will take advantage if they know they will be given extra time to finish. One way to solve the problem is to include a variety of non-graded, content graded, and content-mechanics graded activities.

Non-graded (free) writing means "spelling doesn't count." Students do not revise their work; they do not "hand" it in, and, of course, it is not graded. Non-graded assignments are best kept short in both time of writing and length of writing. Students must write continuously for the specified time. Volunteers may read their compositions aloud, but only positive comments should be made by the teacher and fellow students.

Content-graded writing is usually writing done in one class period and turned in at the end of the period. Students may revise, but they do not have time to rewrite. The content and structure is analyzed by the teacher. Sometimes the writing will be rewritten during the next class period.

Content-mechanics graded (formal) writing assignments are usually finished outside the classroom, or carried over at least two days. The emphasis is on content (ideas) and mechanics (organization, punctuation, structure, spelling, clarity, etc.) and is, of course, revised and rewritten and graded.

Some writing assignments may be read aloud periodically in class for any number of reasons: students are "stuck" and need suggestions; they need reassurance that they are on the right track; they need to know if what they have written is coherent to an audience. Students should arrange ahead of time to read their works-in-progress. If several need to be done, students may be divided into groups to help each other.

The writing process involves three general stages—prewriting, writing, and rewriting. Prewriting covers deciding on a subject, thinking about the subject, maybe even doing some preliminary research, and organizing the ideas, usually in outline form. Writing is putting the words down on paper. Rewriting is revising and reworking what has been written; it is the stage where the writing is cleaned, tightened, and made ready for the eyes of others. The three stages are not separate and distinct from each other; they overlap and shade into each other. All three stages are vital and essential parts of the writing process; any skimping on any of the three stages will be evident in the final product.

Creativity flourishes more easily in a classroom environment of support and acceptance. The right kind of praise—praise for what students do, not for what or who they are—is also important. Avoid evaluating students instead of their work. Deal specifically with what students write and point out the strong points before dealing with the weak.

Students need good, solid, concrete advice on what and how to improve. Point out the areas that need improvement and then make suggestions on how students may improve their writing.

Writing is usually done alone; it is actually a lonely undertaking, so help your students get reinforcement by arranging for them to share their work in a variety of ways—oral readings in class or at other places, productions of school literary magazines, writing contests, and publications in other sources, such as newspapers and magazines. Recognition of good writing is one of the best motivators.

The best thing you can do for your students is to stimulate their imaginations, instill in them a love and appreciation of language, provide them with a solid base in vocabulary and mechanics, and then...let them write.

On the following pages are some tips and suggestions to help you teach writing. They are in no particular order. Pick and choose those that suit your teaching style; adapt and change anything you need to and ignore those that will not work for you. Do not forget...your students are excellent sources of ideas!

Warm-up Activities

Creatively designed and imaginatively executed warm-up activities can play an important part in helping free students' imaginations. They serve to get students to think and to get them excited and involved in the writing process. They should make students want to get started putting their ideas down on paper.

Warm-up activities should be short. I would suggest not exceeding ten minutes. Actually, five minutes can be enough time to devote to some warm-up activities. Warm-up activities should not be used every day. If they are, they lose some of their effectiveness.

BRAINSTORMING

Brainstorming is used to generate as many ideas as possible. It can be used as a whole class activity, in small groups, or individually. Brainstorming may be used with many of the warm-up activities that will be described in this section.

The Basic Rules of Brainstorming

1. Go for quantity. Generate as many ideas as possible.

2. Free-wheeling and absurd or wild ideas are encouraged.

3. Do not evaluate or censor ideas at this time; that can be done later.

4. Use the ideas of others to help generate new ideas. Combine ideas and improve ideas.

5. Questions may be asked to clarify an idea.

6. Discussions, sometimes heated, may ensue.

7. Ten minutes is usually enough time. The first ideas are usually the obvious, while the later ideas tend to be more original, flexible, and elaborate. Do not stop at ten minutes if good ideas are still being generated.

8. All ideas must be recorded; make arrangements ahead of time for them to be taped or written.

ORAL COMPOSITION

Oral composition allows students to talk through an idea before they begin putting words on paper. It allows them a chance to brainstorm divergent ideas before selecting the ones they want to use, and, when used effectively by teachers, it can help students define where they want to go with their writing before they start writing. Some students, however, are resistant to oral composition, feeling that they can do better by just starting to write. Give them a chance to participate, but do try to accomodate the different writing styles of your students.

GROUP ORAL COMPOSITION

Group oral composition can take many forms and many directions; however, I am going to describe briefly an exercise which I have used with students in grades 4-12 and found successful on all eight grade levels.

I define a character in sketchy details to the class. (A committee of students could do this ahead of time and present their creation to the class.) Sometimes I give a situation and setting, sometimes not, but I do set certain rules such as:

1. The story cannot end until I say it may.

2. There cannot be excessive violence. Any violence must be a logical outgrowth of the characters and plot and cannot be the easy solution to a problem.

3. All students must contribute to the story when it is their turn.

After students are presented with the character(s), situation, and setting, I call on the first student (volunteers at first, later some students may need to be encouraged). I give the student the first word on my prepared list of words, and the student then begins the story by working the word into the story line. As the teacher, you will need to pace the story; you should be able to tell when it is time to move on the the next student, who, in turn, gets a new word. It is usually better to keep the tempo fast.

The story may be continued for several class periods as a warm-up activity. Usually some students will want to write what has been created, reinterpret it, and use it for class work. I encourage them to do so.

Following are a suggested character, a situation, a setting, and a list of words. You probably would do better to create your own to suit your own situation.

Character: Tat is a white German shepherd, five years old, friendly, intelligent, and, to dog-lovers, loveable.

Situation: Tat has been dognapped by two inept dog thieves, Joe and Zoe, a married couple.

Setting: Present. Your town.

Words: Siren, baseball field, the mayor, turnip greens, fire trucks, photographer, a ham bone, a bee, a butterfly, a swimming pool, a copy of *Gone with the Wind*, a lawnmower, an oriental vase, an artist, the mayor again, a baby, Bill Cosby, the school principal, a radio, a clock, a newspaper, the artist again, the fire trucks again, a jogger, a Baby Ruth candy bar, a water fountain, a pair of tweezers. (Add to or delete.)

RANDOM WORDS

Choose four words, which may or may not be related in some way. Give the four words to your students and have them compose a paragraph in which they use all four words correctly and in context. Have them list the words at the top of the page for your reference.

Caution: You **must** advise the students that they cannot write: (Teacher) told us to use a paragraph using _____, _____, _____, and _____ or I drew _____, _____, _____, and _____ from the box and I must write a paragraph using them.

PICTURES, PAINTINGS, SCULPTURE AND OTHER ART WORKS

Use pictures, paintings, and other art works to motivate students. Non-representational pictures or paintings can often arouse more interest than representational ones do.

MUSIC

Music may be used in many ways with creative writing. Most students have strong musical preferences, some even to the point of being "closed-minded" about other forms of music. Controversy over musical interests and tastes can be stimulating and can provide subject matter for writing.

A simple warm-up exercise using music is to play several short selections from a variety of musical periods and styles. After each selection, have students write one sentence describing how the music affects them. This activity is highly subjective and, of course, there is no right or wrong response.

SONGS AND POEMS

Songs and poems, like music and art, are useful in getting students to respond. Use all types to elicit varying responses.

PHYSICAL MOVEMENT

Physical movement wakes up sluggish students and stirs the creative muse. Simple stretching exercises will suffice; however, rhythmic exercises, done in beats of four, might prove more popular.

Examples: 1. Stomp, clap, stomp, clap
              2. Clap, snap, clap, snap

Physical movement warm-ups should be used to loosen inhibitions. The exercises must be controlled and never allowed to become ends within themselves. The cheerleaders at your school will probably be happy to develop some routines for you and your students. Just ask.

Journals, Diaries, and Notebooks

Students can create their own written history by keeping a journal or diary. A journal or diary is an account of events, transactions, or observations or a record of experiences, ideas, or reflections kept regularly for private use. Journal or diary entries should always be dated with the day, the month, and the year given. The place of writing should also be noted. Students may purchase diaries and journals or they may make their own using notebooks. Most writers prefer notebooks because they can make the entries as long as they wish.

Students should be encouraged to include in their journals descriptions of typical days and events as well as descriptions of unusual days and events. Following is a list of things that students might wish to include in their journals:

Where I go

What I do

Whom I see

What I say

What they say

How I feel about. . .

What I think about. . .

My reactions to. . .

Plans

What's popular in music, dance, dress, slang, TV, radio, movies, comic books, magazines, etc.

Current events

Character sketches of relatives and friends

Descriptions of favorite authors, athletes, musicians, literary characters, etc.

I require students to write at least three pages of original writing every three weeks in their journals. Journals are read by me, comments made, and the journals are then returned to the students. The more interesting journal entries are generally read aloud to the rest of the class by the students who wrote them. Journals may receive an automatic A if they are turned in on schedule and if they contain three pages of original writing. (You may prefer journals to be non-graded, but, if you do, be prepared to deal with the slow-pokes and no-shows.)

My students have used journal entries for a regular column in our local newspaper. You might check into the possibility of doing the same with your school newspaper or with your local newspaper.

Notebooks may be used in lieu of journals or in addition to journals. If you must make a choice between journals and notebooks, you probably should decide in favor of notebooks. Notebooks should be used to record a variety of bits and pieces which may be used for other writing assignments.

Decide ahead of time what you will require students to include in their notebooks, but allow them the leeway to add other categories. The following is a list of possible inclusions:

Words and expressions

Interesting names (people, places, animals)

Descriptions of people

Descriptions of events

Descriptions of places

Descriptions of actions and mannerisms

Feelings

Opinions

Dreams

Likes and dislikes

Remembrances

Ideas

Others:

Notebooks serve as resources for students when they are writing. Notebooks must be added to constantly, and while they will contain the same categories, they will become highly personal as they continue to grow. Since students never know when something interesting should be recorded, they should have their notebooks with them whenever possible. In any case, it is absolutely necessary that students always have their notebooks with them in writing class since a well kept notebook soon becomes the student writer's most valuable resource.

Writing Activities

The following writing activities should be adapted by you to suit the writing level of your students. Pick and choose, combine and modify these activities any way you please to make them fit your own particular situation. Students can and should make other suggestions which you will want to incorporate into your lesson plans.

LITERATURE

Find examples of great, good, mediocre, and poor passages of literature and copy them. Bring the examples to class and have students analyze them using criteria that you develop as a class. Then have students write their own passages, patterned as much as they are able after the original. Do not overlook the potential for humor in this assignment. This assignment may be used several times during the course.

SIGHT DEPRIVATION

This activity can be done inside the classroom or at other locations. It can be a take-home assignment so that students may choose their own sites. Students blindfold themselves so that they can see nothing. Students use pen and paper or a tape recorder to record their observations, reactions, thoughts, and feelings during the pre-set time. After the blindfold is removed, they analyze and then summarize their conclusions.

SOUND DEPRIVATION

This activity is the same as "Sight Deprivation," but all sounds are filtered out with ear plugs or cotton. In other respects follow the same directions listed above in "Sight Deprivation."

TOASTS

Find a book of toasts and bring it to class to share with your students. After reading enough to establish what constitutes an acceptable toast, have students write toasts for specific individuals, such as a famous rock star, the principal, an author, fellow students, or others.

UNFINISHED DIALOGUE

Write a short unfinished converation between two characters. Tape the dialogue and play it in class or have two students read it aloud. Then have students develop characters and a situation around what they have heard. Two examples of incomplete dialogue follow, but you can probably write better.

Dialogue 1:

First speaker: That's the truth. I swear it.

Second speaker: I don't know. Somehow it doesn't ring true. Maybe you should lie instead of telling the truth. Lying just might be more believable.

First speaker: What do you have in mind?

Second speaker: Well, you know, the part about the rabbit. That is pretty far-fetched. Also, the thing about the lawn mower, well—

First speaker: I know, I know, but I've always thought that honesty was the best policy.

Second speaker: Yeah, yeah. But listen to this—

Dialogue 2:

First speaker: Did you get it?

Second speaker: Of course, I got it.

First speaker: Did you have any trouble?

Second speaker: Darn right, I did. I almost got caught. Not once, but twice. Next time you can jolly well get it for yourself.

First speaker: You know I wouldn't ask you if I could manage to do it myself.

Second speaker: I know. I'm just nervous because it was so close and I don't know what would happen if you—

22

PEOPLE OBSERVATION

Have students go to a place where there are crowds of people passing through, such as a shopping mall or an airport. Have them observe people as they pass by, jotting down information or using a tape recorder to record information about the most interesting ones. This exercise works well when students work in pairs but do not share their observations with each other until they return to class. It is interesting to see the similarities and differences in what they find interesting and the way they interpret what they see.

This activity can be an exercise in observation and accurate recording of selected details and can be an end within itself; however, there are a variety of writing activities which are logical outgrowths. It gives you an excellent opportunity to deal with the uses of selection and condensation in writing with your students. If the activity has been done in pairs, you should already have several examples of selection and condensation from which to choose.

To take the activity one step further, have students choose a person, a couple, or a group they observed and create a background for them. You might have the students determine what kinds of information should be developed in the background information. Next, have the students create a situation explaining why the people they have chosen are passing through, and last, have students explain what happens next to their people.

Another follow-up involves combining students in small groups. They take the materials they have developed around their people and combine the details into a story where all the people meet and interact in some way.

SHORT TRIP

Take students for a short trip outside. Have them select a scene by boxing their hands to form a frame. Have them study the scenes they choose carefully. Then return to the classroom and have them write a description of what they have observed. You might like to follow up by returning to the scenes they have described and having them read their descriptions aloud at the scene. This way they can see what they overlooked or forgot. Variations of this activity can be done several times during the course. Students should become more competent observers as the course progresses.

HOROSCOPES AND FORTUNE COOKIES

Horoscopes and fortune cookies can be good jumping off motivators, and, of course, the cookies may be eaten after the fortunes are removed and read.

LETTERS

Letters and notes are often overlooked as writing activities, but they can be good starting activity, especially with younger students. The advice columnist, Abigail Van Buren, has written a booklet, **How to Write Letters for All Occasions**, which you can order. Check your newspaper for the address and instructions on how to order the booklet. Students might like to have their own copies; give them the necessary information so that they may order for themselves.

Letter writing may be expanded to include pen pals from around the world. Check in your library for a source of addresses.

BOOK REPORTS

Book reports offer an opportunity to teach students very structured writing, or they can be used for imaginative, innovative writing assignments. Over many years of teaching, I have found the following structure for book reports to work well:

Paragraph 1: Include the title of the book, the name of the author, the type of the book, the setting (both time and place), and the original publication date.

Paragraph 2: Include a list of and a brief description of the main characters.

Paragraph 3: Include a brief plot description.

Paragraph 4: Include an evaluation and recommendation.

I limit book reports to no more than two pages. This activity assures that students write about what they know—the books that they have read—and that they learn to work within a structure for both subject matter and length.

GROUP-CREATED STORIES

Create group stories using the following process:

1. Divide students into groups of four.

2. Have each of the four students select one of the following tasks:
    • Create a main character
    • Create supporting characters
    • Create a setting and background and a basic situation
    • Create a crisis, conflict(s), and complications

3. After students have completed the above tasks, which they have done individually, they are to combine the materials they have created and write one of the following:
    • A short story
    • A radio script
    • A play
    • A poem
    • A song
    • A comic strip
    • A newspaper, radio, or TV news story

SUGGESTION BOX

Keep a suggestion box for students. Students must sign their suggestions, which may include story starters, story enders, story ideas, and other suggestions for writing activities. Use the ones that are creative and imaginative.

Notes

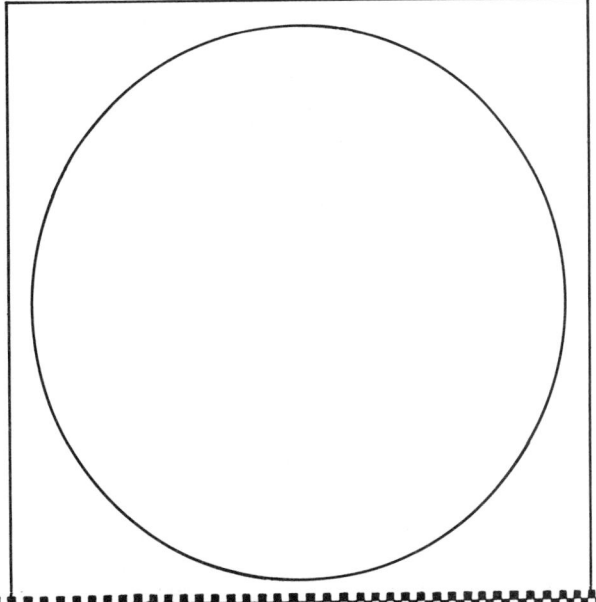

DO NOT DISTURB!

Creative Work Going On

Part II

Student Activity Worksheets

Teacher Directions

The following forty writing activities have been roughly divided into four inexact categories. There is nothing magical in their order or category, so rearrange them any way you need to in order to get the best writing results from your students.

Activities #1-#9 consist of short writing activities. Many of these activities will make good warm-up exercises. These nine activities are like spices—best used in small amounts—so do not work through all nine one after the other, but instead, sprinkle them throughout the year.

Activities #10-#13 are mainly "what if" exercises, which ask students to think in terms of what would happen if a known and/or stable condition should change.

Activities #14-#25 ask students to draw from their personal experiences to develop writing topics.

Activities #26-#40 are story ideas and story starters.

Barefoot Sensations
Activity #1

Describe the following sensations with exact, colorful language.

Walking Barefoot . . .

On Spilled Sugar   **At the Edge of the Ocean**

On Hot Sand   **In the Snow**

In Sandspurs   **On Deep Pile Carpet**

Barefoot Sensations
Activity #1
continued

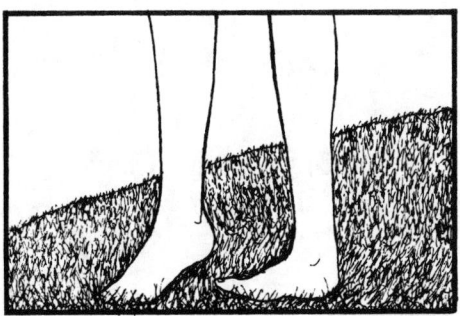

On Sun-warmed Just-cut Grass

On Rose Petals   In Mud

On Cold Tile   On Hot Coals

Sensations: Sounds
Activity #2

Describe the following sounds with colorful, exact language.

The Sound of . . .

**A Grandfather Clock
In an Empty House**

A Much-loved Voice on the Phone

Crickets and Frogs on a Summer Night

**The Ring of the Phone
When You're Lonely**

A Siren

A Dog Howling Late at Night

Sensations: Sounds
Activity #2
continued

The Sound of Your Parent's Car
When He/She Comes Home

A Loaded School Bus

Your Mother or Father Calling
You to Get Up on a Cold Morning

Thunder

Your House During Dinner

Sensations: Smells
Activity #3

Describe the following odors with colorful, exact language.

The Smell of . . .

Bread Baking

Your Favorite Perfume

A Garbage Dump

Popcorn Popping

Onions Frying

The Interior of a New Car

Sensations: Smells
Activity #3
continued

Coffee Perking

Chlorine Bleach

A Just-bathed Baby

A Hospital

Spring

Sensations: Sight
Activity #4

Describe the following sights with colorful, exact language.

The Sight of . . .

A Basketball Game

A Mother Bird Feeding Her Babies

Goldfish in an Outdoor Pool

A Beautiful Spring Garden

Your Favorite House

The Halls in Your School at Class Breaks

Sensations: Sight
Activity #4
continued

A Baby Learning to Walk

A Party   **A Dog Swimming in the Lake**

Your Bedroom   **A Pep Rally**

Sensations: Taste
Activity #5

Describe the tastes of the following items. Use colorful, exact language to create a taste sensation.

The Taste of . . .

A Cola

Fresh Strawberries

A Lemon

An Apple

Yoghurt

Potato Chips

Sensations: Taste
Activity #5
continued

Pizza

A Chili Hotdog with Sauerkraut

Ice Cream

Creamy Mashed Potatoes

Popcorn

Sensations: Touch
Activity #6

Use colorful, exact language to describe the feel of the following things.

The Feel of . . .

A Kitten

A Fire on a Cold Day

Concrete Block Walls

Sand (Wet and Dry)

A Cool Breeze after a Hot Tennis Game

Corduroy

Sensations: Touch
Activity #6
continued

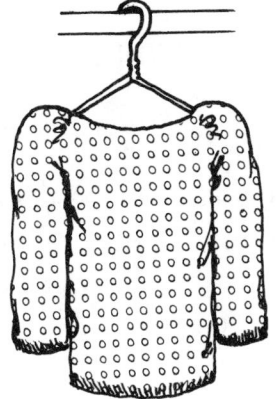

A Favorite Sweater

Your Face

Mud between Your Toes

A Hug from Your Mother
When You Need Comfort

Walking in the Rain
(Give the Circumstances)

Reactions
Activity #7

How would you react if the following happened to you?

Situation #1:

You are in your new, best clothes having dinner with someone very important at a classy restaurant. The waiter spills a plate of food on you.

Situation #2:

It is your birthday, but no one seems to notice or care.

Situation #3:

You are tossing a ball with your brother in the living room, an activity strictly forbidden by your parents, when your brother misses his catch. The ball crashes into the new crystal lamp your father gave your mother for their last wedding anniversary. The lamp breaks.

Situation #4:

You are visiting a friend. The family has a bad-tempered little mutt, which you detest, but your friend and his family adore him. The mutt will not stop tormenting you.

Patterns
Activity #8

One synonym for pattern is design. One of the many definitions of pattern is a natural or chance or purposeful configuration. Patterns in the natural environment are asymmetrical; man-made patterns may be either asymmetrical or symmetrical. Describe the following patterns using language to make your readers ''see'' and ''feel'' the patterns.

Sunlight Filtering Through an Apple Tree

A Baseball Diamond

The Knitted Design of a Sweater

A Flower Garden in Moonlight

A Lace Shawl

Ivy Growing on an Old Brick Wall

First Impressions
Activity #9

Our first impressions of people often change as we get to know them better. Describe your first impressions of the following people and explain how these impressions have changed over time. You may make substitutions if you want to.

Your dentist:

A teacher:

Your best friend:

A relative:

A friend of your parents:

Creations
Activity #10

What kind of masterpiece would you like to create? Which field—art, music, dance, drama, architecture, literature, engineering, for instance—would you choose? Why? Describe the masterpiece and tell what you would hope to achieve with your creation.

Inventions
Activity #11

"Why doesn't someone invent _____?" is a question we hear and probably even ask occasionally. It sometimes seems that if only someone would invent a simple machine to perform a certain function, then all our lives would be much easier.

In the space below identify a need for an invention; tell how you would invent, manufacture, and market the invention, and describe the benefits of the invention.

Second-guessing
Activity #12

If the airplane and the television had been invented and in wide use before the Revolutionary War, how might their widespread use have prevented the war and changed the history of the United States?

A United Earth
Activity #13

The year is 2096. There is now a one-world government on Earth, which is organized somewhat like the government of the United States was during your lifetime. What were separate countries during the twentieth century are now organized and governed somewhat like the states in the United States were, with the final power resting with the one-world government, which is a democracy. There is an official language; it is a combination of English and computer language. There has been peace for many years.

Describe what life is like for your descendants living during 2096. Explain how is it different from the life you lived?

Walk a Mile in My Shoes
Activity #14

You are the shoes of a ballet dancer, a mail carrier, a basketball player, a golfer, a teacher, or a nurse. What is a typical day like for you? What are your activities, thoughts, reactions, and feelings during the course of your day? In the space below write about what happens to you during a typical day and your thoughts, reactions, and feelings about what happens.

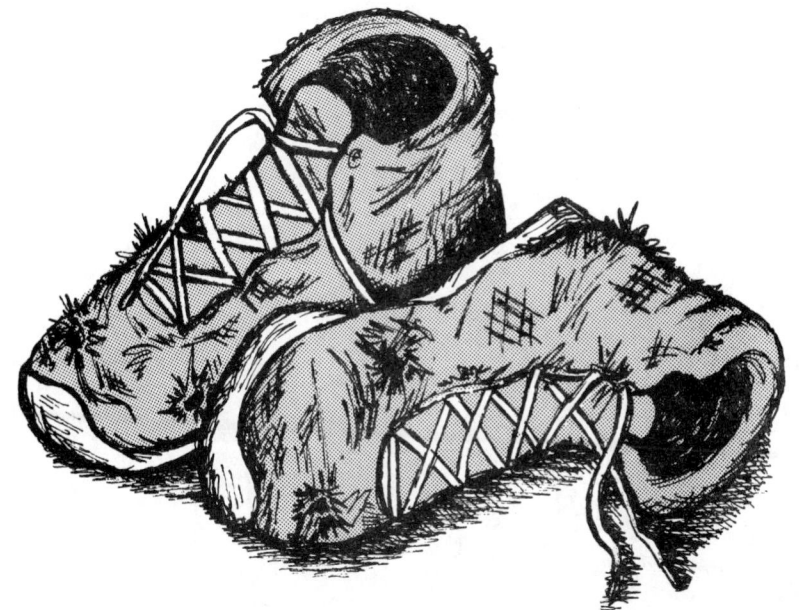

Telephone Booth
Activity #15

You are a telephone booth in a major airport, a hotel lobby, your school, a grocery store, at a busy street corner, or some other busy location. Who uses you? What do you hear? How are you treated? How do you feel about your role in life? In the space below write all the facts the public needs to know about the life of a telephone booth.

I Am a _____

Activity #16

Imagine you are a bicycle (or some other vehicle). Describe yourself. Tell who has owned you and how you have been treated. How did it feel to be stolen, left out in the rain and snow, or run over in the drive? How did it feel to be a new surprise? How did it feel to be ridden on a gravel drive, on hot pavement, in the snow, or in the rain? How did it feel to get new air put in your tires or to be loaded down with too many passengers? How does it feel now to be discarded because your owner has become old enough to drive a car?

Balloon
Activity #17

You are a balloon in a bunch held by a little girl, who has been given the bunch of balloons for her birthday. She is running with you and your fellow balloons in the park when she falls and lets you go. Suddenly you are free and floating higher and higher and further and further away from the little girl. A gust of wind carries you even higher and further away and now you're on your own.

Where do you go? What do you see? What do you smell, hear, and taste? How do you feel? How do things appear from so high up? (Remember perspective.) What finally happens? Why? How do you feel about your adventure?

Decisions, Decisions
Activity #18

All day long you make decisions. Many of the decisions you make are fairly routine—what to wear or what to have for lunch, for example; however, all of us, sooner or later, face tougher decisions than the routine, day-to-day ones—decisions which may have long-lasting consequences. What is the hardest decision you have ever made? What were the short-range effects? What were the long-range effects? If you could make the decision over, would you make the same decision? Why or why not?

Stage Fright
Activity #19

Has your mind ever gone totally blank when you had an audience? Have your fingers and/or lips ever gone stiff at a music recital? Have your legs ever turned to jelly on the playing field? Stage fright is a malady which seems to strike just about everyone sooner or later. In the space below describe your bout(s) with stage fright. Make your readers suffer with you as you describe your ordeal in excruciating detail. A story of this type needs a "snappy" and, if possible, upbeat ending—an ending which relieves some of the embarrassing pain the writer and reader have just suffered.

What I Do Because I Must
Activity #20

If doing those things which are necessary, even when they are distasteful, helps create a strong character, then my character should really be strong by now because I do two things every day which I dislike—I go to bed at night and I get up in the morning. What are some things you **must** do which you dislike doing? Why do you dislike doing them? Why must you do them? What are some strategies which you have already developed or might develop to help you?

Answer the above questions in an essay. You might like to limit yourself to just one thing which you dislike doing.

Mornings
Activity #21

What is a typical school morning like at your house? Describe a specific morning or a typical morning in the space below. Attempt to capture the total atmosphere by describing sights, smells, sounds, tastes, textures, tempos, feelings, actions, reactions, conversations, and attitudes. If Saturday and/or Sunday mornings are very different, you might like to describe one or both to show a contrast.

Changes
Activity #22

For one day only you have been granted the ability to change one thing. You may choose to change one thing about yourself, your family, your home, the environment, your community, your state, your country, or the world, but it can only be one thing, and once the change has occurred, it is irreversible. What would you choose to change? Why? What might the short range and long range consequences of the change be?

Games
Activity #23

Most people enjoy playing games. In the space below identify your favorite game and tell how you first became interested in it. Next, describe the circumstances and rules of play in such a way that even a novice could understand and play the game. Finally, tell why you enjoy playing the game and describe any benefits you derive from playing the game? Are there any minuses? If so, weigh them against the benefits and evaluate them.

Best Friend
Activity #24

What is a friend? Give a dictionary definition first and then your own definition of what a friend is. Next identify and describe your best friend.

According to my dictionary, a friend is _____

_____

_____

My definition of a friend is _____

_____

_____

Who is your best friend?

Why is this person your best friend?

Describe your best friend.

Ideal Friend
Activity #25

What is an ideal friend? Describe your idea of what an ideal friend would be like.

Write a paragraph telling why you would or would not make an ideal friend.

Discoveries
Activity #26

What is the most important discovery that you have ever made or the most important thing that you have ever learned? How has it affected your life and thus the lives of those close to you?

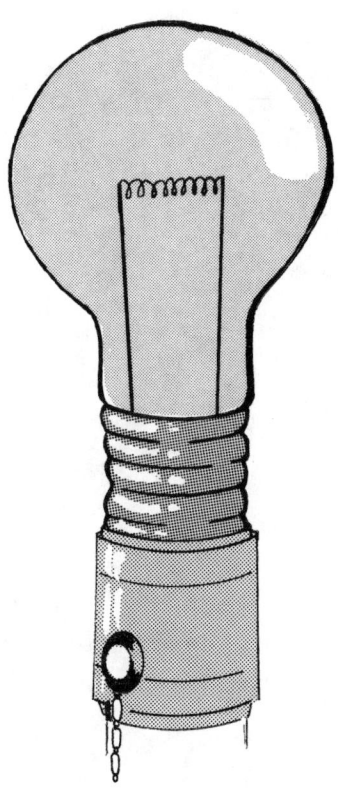

Promises
Activity #27

Complete the following story starter:

PROMISES

The day stepped out of the calendar dressed in its new spring outfit. It was a diamond-and-emerald studded day, a day to be savored to the fullest, packed away in rose petals, and then treasured forever. On a day like this, I thought, I can do anything; I can be anything.

Perceptions
Activity #28

When I was growing up in Crenshaw County, Alabama, I had an aunt who was fond of saying, "It's not the things you see in the mirror that count; it's what you look like turned inside out." What do you think she meant when she said that? Write a short story demonstrating the truth of my aunt's statement.

The Pink and Yellow Frog
Activity #29

Complete the following story by telling . . .
  1. Why only Heather can help the frog,
  2. How Heather can help the frog,
  3. How Heather helps the frog, and
  4. How it all ends.

The Pink and Yellow Frog
Activity #29
continued

THE PINK AND YELLOW FROG

One sunny May day Heather was skipping home from school. She took a short detour through the park. As she skipped around the lily pond for the second time, she heard, ''Heather, Heather.''

Heather looked around, but she saw no one. Puzzled, she shook her head and started to skip away. ''No, wait, Heather. Look in the lily pond,'' she heard.

Heather stopped and approached the lily pond slowly. She saw a yellow and pink frog sitting on a lily pad.

The frog spoke to her again. ''Heather, only you can help me.''

Alec Through the TV Screen
Activity #30

The following is a story idea and should be expanded to become the first part of your story. Take what has been provided and rewrite it dramatically by showing actions, reactions, thoughts, and conversations as they occur. Then develop the story all the way to an ending.

Alec was watching his favorite television show (you provide the name of the show) one night. All of a sudden there was a **WHOOSH!** and Alec found himself inside the TV set. It took him a while to realize that he was now the main character in the story he'd been watching—not Alec playing the actor playing the character, nor the actor playing the character, but the character himself. (Alec may be male or female.)

A New Reading Experience
Activity #31

Complete the following story which has been started for you.

_____
(Title)

I checked out *Treasure Island*, by Robert Louis Stevenson, from the library. When I got it home and started to read it, I discovered an envelope in it addressed to "Next Reader."

I decided that I must be "Next Reader," so I opened the envelope. What a surprise awaited me!

I Won a Camel
Activity #32

Complete the following story.

I WON A CAMEL

My mother was busy when the doorbell rang. She asked me to answer it. When I opened the door, I saw two men holding a large chain. At the end of the chain stood a camel winking at me.

"We are delivering the prize you won in the Save the Animals Contest. Enjoy it!" they said as they handed me the end of the chain.

"Wait a minute," I yelled as they got in their very large truck and drove away. "I didn't enter any contest." But they were already out of sight.

"Mother!" I yelled.

I Won a Camel

A Wiggling Surprise
Activity #33

Rewrite the following story idea and then complete the story.

One morning you rush out your front door to catch the school bus. You spy a bundle on the top step just in time to avoid stepping on it. You hastily pull your foot back and stoop to get a better look. It is wiggling and making a funny noise.

Why Harmony Was Misnamed
Activity #34

Write a short story that goes with the title, "Why Harmony Was Misnamed." Write a beginning where you introduce your main character and the situation. Follow with the middle part of the story where you develop your characters and the situation. End with a strong finish.

WHY HARMONY WAS MISNAMED

An Unappreciated Gift
Activity #35

For your birthday your favorite aunt, Aunt Susie, gave you an expensive, but absolutely awful, outfit. What are your options? How might you deal with the situation? In the space below list your options.

An Unappreciated Gift
Activity #35
continued

Think about the options you just listed. Choose the best option and write a scenario (an account or synopsis of a projected course of action or events) about what will probably happen if you follow through on this course of action.

Newspaper Stories
Activity #36

You are a reporter for your school newspaper. Your adviser has just given you a list of possible topics for your next story. Choose one of those topics, which are listed below, and write an entertaining and informative story about it.

Schools Closed Friday

Big Changes Coming in the Lunchroom

Final Exams Cancelled

Two-hour Breaks Planned

Surprise Assembly Planned for Monday

Friendly Letter
Activity #37

Write a letter to a friend. Your teacher will review the structure of a friendly letter with you. In the letter, tell your friend about your school schedule and activities, your friends, your hobbies and interests, your family, and your plans for summer vacation.

Winning Ways
Activity #38

Have you ever won anything, such as a prize or a contest? If so, what? What were the circumstances? How did you feel about your win? What did you do with what you won? Write a story about your win. If you have never won anything, write your story as if you won a small puppy in the "Adopt an Animal" contest sponsored by your local Humane Society.

A Visitor From the Past
Activity #39

If you could choose any historical figure to come visit you in your home, whom would you choose? How would you prepare for the visit? How would you entertain your guest? What would you discuss? What questions would you ask? What would you want to tell your guest? What would you want to show or demonstrate to your guest? Why? How would the visit end? In the space below describe the visit.

An Important Visitor
Activity #40

If you could choose anyone now living to come visit you, whom would you choose? Why? What would you do to entertain your important visitor? How would you behave? What would you discuss? What questions would you ask? What would you want to tell and/or show your guest? Would you ask for any special favors from your guest? If so, what? In the space below describe the visit.